An Address to All the Colored Citizens of the United States

I0080906

**PREPARED FOR PUBLICATION
BY**
HISTORIC PULISHING

All Rights Reserved. No part of this publication may be reproduced, stored in a retrieval system, or transmitted, in any form, or by any means, electronic, mechanical, photocopying, recording, or otherwise, without the prior consent of the publisher.

HISTORIC PULISHING
©2017 (Edited Materials)

HISTORIC PULISHING
All Rights Reserved.
©2017

An Address to All the Colored Citizens of the United States

John B. Meachum

AN ADDRESS
TO ALL THE
COLORED CITIZENS
OF THE
UNITED STATES.

BY

JOHN B. MEACHUM,
PASTOR OF THE AFRICAN BAPTIST
CHURCH, ST. LOUIS, MO.

Ethiopia shall soon stretch out her hands unto God.-
-PSALM 68, 31.

PHILADELPHIA:
PRINTED FOR THE AUTHOR,
BY KING AND BAIRD.
1846.

[5]

An Address to All the Colored Citizens of the United States

PREFACE.

DEAR FRIENDS:--The author of this little book was born a slave, in Goochland county, Virginia, May 3d, 1789. I belonged to a man by the name of Paul Meachum, who moved to North Carolina, and lived there nine years. He then moved to Hardin county, Kentucky, where I still remained a slave with him. He was a good man and I loved him, but could not feel myself satisfied, for he was very old, and looked as if death was drawing near to him. So I proposed to him to hire my time, and he granted it. By working in a saltpeter cave I earned enough to purchase my freedom.

Still I was not satisfied, for I had left my father in old Virginia, and he was a slave. It seemed to me, at times, though I was seven hundred miles from him, that I held conversation with him, for he was near my heart. However, this did not stop here, for industry will do a great deal. In a short time I went to Virginia, and bought my father, and paid one hundred pounds for him, Virginia money. It was a joyful meeting when we met together, for we had been apart a long time. He was a Baptist preacher, living in Hanover county, and went by the name of Thomas Granger. While there, on a Sunday morning after I had bought the old man, he was singing and my eyes filled with tears. He turned to me and said, "you are yet in your sins." His words went to my heart, and I began to pray and seek the

[8]

Lord. Four weeks from that day I found peace in believing upon the Lord Jesus, related my experience to the church, and was baptized by elder Puritan, in Louisa county. This was in the year 1811, when I was about twenty-one years old. My father and myself then earned enough to pay our expenses on the way, and putting our knapsacks on our backs walked seven hundred miles to Hardin county, Kentucky. Here the old man met his wife and all his children, who had been there several years. Oh there was joy!

In a short time, my mother and all her children received their liberty, of their good old master. My father and his family settled in Harrison county, Indiana.

I married a slave in Kentucky, whose master soon took her to St. Louis, in Missouri. I followed her, arriving there in 1815, with three dollars in my pocket. Being a carpenter and cooper I soon obtained business, and purchased my wife and children. Since that period, I have purchased about twenty slaves, most of whom paid back the greatest part of the money, and some paid all. They are all free at this time, and doing well, excepting one, who happened to be a drunkard, and no drunkard can do well. One of the twenty colored friends that I bought is worthy to be taken notice of, to show what industry will do. I paid for him one thousand dollars. He worked and paid back the thousand dollars. He has also bought a lot of ground for which he paid a thousand dollars. He married a slave and bought her, and paid seven hundred dollars for her. He has built a house that cost him six hundred dollars. He is a blacksmith, and has worked for one man ever since he has been in St. Louis. So much for industry.

I commenced preaching in 1821, and was ordained as a minister of the gospel in 1825. From that time to this, I have been the pastor of the African Baptist Church in St. Louis, which has now more than five hundred members. The Sunday school has an attendance from one hundred and fifty to three hundred.

I have written this little book to show you the great desire I have for the welfare of this people. I hope each colored person will read this with a great deal of care, knowing it is for your welfare, both soul and body. My dear friends, I have been looking at the long distance this people is behind others, and it makes my soul mourn their sad state. I will tell you what I have been thinking of,--I have thought it likely that this people is away from home, and God hath got a place somewhere that they can see great comfort and satisfaction. And so friends, let us become united, and keep in union against the time comes.

Do not look at this little book with a careless eye, but receive instruction and advice. I want you to take notice that Israel started very fair for the promised land, all minds bent the way God told them to go. But they rebelliously turned back in heart, and God left them to wander in the wilderness till all the old heads died, excepting Caleb and Joshua. It was only about forty days journey in a straight course, but God made them wander forty years before they reached Canaan. So, my friends, we may start fair for this union, and a great many may turn back in heart, and never enter the promised land. He that puts his hand to the plough and looks back is not fit for the kingdom.

My heart is enlarged for the welfare of this people. I wish them to be industrious and religious in their feelings. If UNION is God Almighty's plan, let us hasten to it. The blessing of God will rest upon us. But we may reject the council of the Father of Light and Knowledge to our hurt.

Be faithful unto death, and you shall have a crown of life.

JOHN B. MEACHUM.

St. Louis, August, 1846.

An Address to All the Colored Citizens of the United States

ADDRESS.

Psalm 133, 1st verse. "Behold, how good and how pleasant it is for brethren to dwell together in unity!"

PROVIDENCE has placed us all on the shores of America--and God has said, "Ethiopia shall soon stretch out her hands unto God." Psalm 68, 31.

This being true, is it not necessary that some exertion should be made? Ought we not to use our influence and the means placed in our power for the consummation of this end. All will admit that we are capable of elevating ourselves, for we have once been distinguished as one of the greatest nations, and it is reasonable to suppose that what has once been can be again. Sin has degraded us, but righteousness will exalt us. We are under positive moral obligations to effect this object, by our religious influence, by mental culture, and by appropriating a portion of our worldly goods to the accomplishment of this end. Should we willfully neglect embracing the facilities and means we have of effecting this object, it will be said to us on the final day of accounts, "depart from me, for ye knew your duty and did it not."

I now proceed to state by what means we came to America, and the cause of our degradation as a people. History informs us that the first inhabitants of America who came from Africa were transported

[13]

from Guinea. Las Casas, who was a great friend to the Indians, who were then forced to work in mines by the Spaniards, interposed, and had these Africans forced to do that which the Indians had been compelled to do. The Indians therefore were released from bondage entirely, and the Africans made to substitute them. Thus you perceive he enslaves one nation to liberate the other. Strange benevolence this, that he should employ so much of his time and influence in securing liberty to the Indians, while at the same time he made every possible effort to reduce the African to the same state of servitude! He went so far as to go to Spain and procure a grant for the transportation of four thousand negroes in order to secure to the Indians their personal rights and freedom.

About 1620 a Dutch vessel brought African slaves to the colony of Jamestown, Virginia.

Our people had war among themselves in Africa. They brought with them the same principles here,--envy, hatred, malice, jealousy. The principles, which they possessed, originated doubtless, from ignorance and from the fact that they belonged to separate kingdoms and fought against each other while there, and consequently retained the same feelings of hostility and enmity abroad.

God has formed man out of clay, and all nations have sprung therefrom. It is therefore not natural for man to hate his fellow, but it is to be traced to other causes. Shall we then who are of the same species, same color, &c., cultivate and cherish a principle so contrary to reason and scripture, and in its consequences so direful and disastrous?

Our people can only distinguish themselves as a nation by "fearing God," and "working righteousness," for "righteousness exalteth a nation, but sin is a reproach to any people." We must therefore be united in love and affection--our interests, aims, and hopes must be one--for in the language of the text, "Behold how good and how pleasant it is for brethren to dwell together in unity!" We must cultivate all the Christian graces, which the apostle Peter recommends--"add to your faith virtue, and to virtue knowledge, and to knowledge temperance, and to temperance patience, and to patience godliness, and to godliness brotherly kindness, and to brotherly kindness charity." Upon the exercise of these graces and Christian qualities depend our elevation in this life, and our eternal happiness in the world to come.

We must have union--we can and must have it, else we shall remain in darkness, ignorance and superstition, in a state of moral and intellectual degradation. It is an old maxim with which you are all familiar--"in union there is strength." Again,

[15]

"united we stand, divided we fall." Let us then be of one mind, and one spirit, and cultivate that principle of true benevolence which will exert a wholesome and salutary influence on the world, secure the blessings of God upon us, and benefit our own souls.

Diversity of opinion may exist in regard to the formation of this union. One may assert, I am a Methodist, another, I am a Baptist, and another, I am a Presbyterian, but different persuasions should not prevent our union,--we should not possess any sectarian feeling or party spirit. UNION should be our constant watchword--it should be the standard to which all of us should rally. As in family relations, so in national affairs,--for example, a man and his wife are at variance, they disagree among themselves, but let anything arise pertaining to the interest of the whole family, all minor differences and opinions are forthwith forgotten and they become united as one. Let us then, at this important crisis when a matter is pending which is bearing upon our present and eternal destiny, lose sight of all party spirit and sectarian feelings, and unite in one band of love, for, as says the Psalmist, "Behold how good and how pleasant it is for brethren to dwell together in unity!"

Union must begin among the free, then extend to all. Excuse the remark, I care not where it commence, but it is more in the power of the free to

[16]

promote it than those who are differently situated, and I verily believe that only a portion of the free should be consulted in the outset--they should be men of worth, good, moral, religious, intelligent, influential men, whose only object would be to promote the glory of God and to do good to their fellow men; with such men at the head, great and wonderful things could be accomplished. Moses, for example, did not go to all the Israelites, but to the elders only when he called the people together. I will state some measures or plan by which the elders could assemble themselves together, and devise some method to effect this great and important object. In order to do this, I would propose that a Convention be held at some time and place, and ministers of all denominations be invited to attend, and adopt some measures to attain this point, which if attained will be instrumental in securing for us peace, happiness and liberty.

It is a common thing for people to suppose that our oppression is occasioned by severe restrictions and disabilities laid upon us by others, but the truth is you keep yourselves down, for as long as you continue to speak evil one of the other and use abusive epithets, and backbite, ridicule and reproach one another with opprobrious names, just so long will you be oppressed, for it is an old and true maxim, "if you do not respect yourself others will not respect you."

The term Negro originated from a river in Africa called Niger, but it is now used as a term of reproach by both black and white--we must therefore stop it, for unless we do, others will use and apply those terms to us with impunity. Yea, the great misfortune is that you do not respect yourselves sufficiently; families, societies, religious denominations speak evil one of another, and thereby in a great measure destroy the influence which they might otherwise exert. To sum up all in a few words, "these things ought not so to be."

Many years have elapsed and no general steps have as yet been taken--it is time we were up and doing. We should shake off our lethargy and make the best use of the means we have. In the first place, parents should by no means neglect the education of their children, but should endeavor to instill such principles in them when young as could never be eradicated by time, place, or circumstance.--You are all aware that impressions can be made upon the mind of the child when young which will be as lasting as time itself, for, says Solomon, "train up a child the way he should go and when he is old he will not depart from it." Prov. xxii. 6. We should obey God, for obedience, as saith the scripture, is better than sacrifice. When the children of Israel obeyed Moses, the enemy fell on every side; when disobedient they were conquered by their enemies; We cannot therefore expect to accomplish any thing until we are living in the discharge of every duty

[18]

urged upon us by the Lord, "for success is from the Lord, without him we can do nothing."

When this union of sentiment, feeling and affection is formed and established among us, we can by the organization of societies, the erection of schools and the establishment of colleges, institutions and seminaries of learning, soon arrive to the same scale of being which those who are considered our superiors have attained. We are susceptible of acquiring the same attainments and arriving to the same elevation that others have attained, which can be substantially proved by history or analogy, reason and philosophy. Shall we not, I then ask, attain this end--ought we not? Surely, none will say, Nay. Then let us be united.

Let us well consider these things. Look at the young and rising generation. See the great mass of them growing up without education. What is the reason of this? We answer, because the fathers are not united, and the children growing up without union to the great body of their fellow beings of the same color. The mother hath not taught it to the child, and he has nothing to rouse his mind to action. But et us take it in consideration now and wake up the minds of our children. We are bound by the law of God and man, and our good sense, to train up our children in the way they shall go when young, that when they grow old they should not depart from it. "Love your neighbor as yourself," is

[19]

the command of the New Testament. We are morally bound by the law of God to teach this to our children. Union is love. What father is in the world that cannot teach the child this principle that the Savior hath commanded? Surely, our people have not considered what God hath required of us to do for the young race of people. Our fathers were not able to do anything for us as to education, and we feel the need of it. So, reader let us duly consider what is best for this people and hasten to do it. Union is the strong cord that binds nations together. Then let the mother teach it to the child, and let the father not forget that he is accountable before God for the raising of his children. Recollect that for the faithfulness of Noah God gave him his children to be saved with him. "And the Lord said unto Noah, come thou and all thy house into the ark; for thee have I seen righteous before me in this generation." Genesis vii. 1. Then let us wake up in this matter, that we may be enabled to teach men fully the way to those under our control. Union! oh this lovely union exalts nations and keeps heaven secure. Then let us look around and see how far our people are from being a united people. Now what can we expect if we continue to stand in the same condition,--no union existing among so large a mass of people. The God of heaven is willing for us to be a united people. The Lord Jesus Christ himself says, "how often would I have gathered thy children together, as a hen doth gather her brood under her wings, and ye would not." Luke xiii. 34. Then let us look to him with a full purpose of heart that this union may be effected. We have everything before us. Here are the gospel ministers that cannot teach anything else to their hearers consistent with the doctrines, which they preach, peace and love and union with all men. Now, my brethren, let us look at this matter and see if we are not a great way off from being in union. Still, you say, "you must love one another; this is the good doctrine that God the eternal loves." Then, I ask the reader, why stand you so far from being a united people? The word of God tells us, "ask, and it shall be given you; seek, and ye shall find." Luke xi. 10. And again he tells us, "If any of you lack wisdom, let him ask of God, that giveth to all men liberally, and upbraideth not; and it shall be given him." James i. 5. Have you done it? If you have, then thy heart is clear for this union.

Let the fathers look at our race of people and see if there is not needed a great cultivation in order to bring it to what it ought to be. In the first place they ought to be a united people, and then they should go on with a general education of our race. Looking particularly on the young race, we have a great deal to do. My dear reader, I think we have been asleep ever since we have come into existence, and it is now high time that we should awake out of sleep before we are awakened by the thunders of Jehovah to give account of our stewardship in this world. This nation lost their standing as a people by

[21]

disobedience, and shall we still live in disobedience and not endeavor to cultivate the mind of our people when we see how much it is needed. Let us redeem the time now by coming together and having our hearts warm with this union, that is so completely calculated to do this people good. All of us know what division is, for we have been trying it for many years, and what has been gained by it? I answer, nothing but strife and confusion. Look at it, my friends, and see if God do not require better things of us. Look around again, and see this great nation coming up in the world. There are hundreds of thousands of colored children under sixteen years of age! Will the fathers stand so far distant from each other that this young race of people's case cannot be reached? Are we not recommended by our blessed Lord to be as lights in the world, or as a city set on a hill that cannot be hid. And we are recommended to let the light shine so that others may see our good work and glorify our Father which is in heaven. Understand it well, that these words are not to be looked at by the reader and then thought no more of. Take notice!--Charity begins at home, and these words were spoken by the blessed Savior, and should we not hearken to the voice of God? If we will not hearken to man's words concerning our own welfare, certainly we should pay the strictest attention to the voice of our Creator that made heaven and earth, and formed man for his own glory. I ask the reader, if it would not be to the glory of God for us to endeavor to train up our children in the nurture and admonition of the Lord? Then if you think so, let us feel it a duty enjoined upon every son and daughter of our race, to endeavor to become united, that we may throw our mites together, and have schools in every state and county where the free children are in large numbers. How can this be done, unless we come together as a band of united brethren, and make agreement that we will no longer stand in opposition one against the other, but that our hearts and souls shall be united together. The principle that we have been living under is the old African principle, kingdom against kingdom, and nation against nation. Let every colored citizen wage war against that old African principle that was the means of throwing the first colored man on the American soil. Will you hold that principle any longer that has been your downfall? Come, brethren, let us proclaim union in every breast. Let all become peace-makers. God hath said, "Blessed are the peace-makers, for they shall be called the children of God." Matthew v. 9. I ask, if there be any one among our people who would not say, "let me be a child of God." Then be a peace maker, and be united in love, and just as sure as the words are left on record you shall be called the child of God, "and if children, then heirs; heirs of God, and joint heirs with Christ." Romans viii. 17. There is nothing better than to be called a child of God by the blessed Saviour who knows the hearts of all men. Then let us seek peace with all men. If we attend to these things, the blessing of

[23]

heaven will be upon this large mass of people that hath been so long under the weather. Consider that the God of heaven is righteous, and never will you be a people until you do right. When we look back and view the Israelites when they left their land, there were only about three score and ten souls, and then see the great number that they grew to be. When they left Egypt, there were six hundred thousand men over twenty years of age. The Levites were not numbered with the rest of the Israelites. Then look at the number under twenty years, and you must see that there was a great number. Then look at our number of children that are under sixteen, and see if it does not give a thought that we ought to take this young race in hand, and attend to them faithfully by bringing them up God fearing and God thinking children?

Here is one thing that I shall name to every father or mother, or any head of a family, we should endeavor to raise our children with as much industry as we possibly can. Work never hurts the child. See particularly that they are raised up nicely in their manners and their deportment. It takes a long time to get the training of a child out of him, and if it is good we do not want to get it out of him. In order that we might do more for our young children, I would recommend manual labor schools to be established in the different states, so as the children could have free access to them. And I would recommend in these schools pious teachers,

[24]

either white or colored, who would take all pains with the children to bring them up in piety, and in industrious habits. We must endeavor to have our children look up a little, for they are too many to lie in idleness and dishonor. Just as sure as you see a lazy child, and his parent cannot break that child from his laziness, he is very apt to become a disgrace to his parents and to himself, and not fit for any society. So let us endeavor to keep laziness out of our children; let them be raised up honorable men and women. Honorable, did you say? Yes, and perfectly honest. You never did see a rogue an honorable man. Let the child look at these things himself. If he hath any heart to be an honorable man, he would not be a thief, stealing little things and by and by begin on big things, just as he grows old enough to hide it, as he thinks. But when he thinks all is safe and hid, somebody sees him, and presents him to be tried by the laws of the country; he is found guilty and condemned to the state prison. Not only so, see the whole family disgraced by the conduct of one member of that family. So much, then, for stealing. Always avoid that one thing, and you can be as honorable a man in society as any other industrious man.

Let us attend to the things that are calculated to elevate the colored citizens of America. Every man endeavor to be an honorable man, and then we can have an honorable society. We know that there are some of our people so full of that old African principle that they have no desire that this people should become united that they may be more able to do something for this young race that is coming along so rapidly. We will pull such along if we can, and when we can hold them no longer, we will let them go and renounce them, but have an eye to their children.

I have said much about children, but I have not told all my thoughts about the dear little damsels, so near and dear to the mother. Touch one of them, and you touch her heartstring at once. Then, dear mother, if you love your daughter, show it in doing all you can do for those so near to your bosom. Teach her the right way to live in this world that she may be happy in the world to come. Teach them morality--teach them to be decent and modest in their deportment. Mothers too often let girls go their own way, and they go to their ruin. Let them know that there is one right way. Industry is right, then make them industrious. Do not scold and fret at the children, but counsel them, talk with them a great deal and endeavor to get them to do right. Give them "line upon line, and precept upon precept." When you get through your good advice and find the child still disobedient, then you must give him or her what all disobedient children ought to have in order to let them know that the voice of a mother must be regarded by the child. Never allow the child to tell you a lie, and if you promise him anything keep your word. Having gone through a nice

[26]

conversation with him, mothers are too apt to get in a passion, and in that passion correct the child too severely. Some go so far as to strike them over the head, or knock them to the ground because they are mad. These things ought not so to be. Hold your temper and spare the child till you get right for correction. Recollect that God hath given you that child for his glory and your comfort, and again I tell you that you are accountable to God for the raising of the child.

These things ought to lay near the heart of this people, and see if our senses will not come to us more than heretofore, concerning duties that we owe to God, before we can be anything that we ought to be. Look over the fields that are white and ready for harvest. Come, friends, have union one with the other. O this union! let us try it. Believe God, and see if he will not open the windows of heaven and pour us out such a wonderful blessing that there shall not be room enough to contain it. Now let the little book hunt out the united brethren. Free colored citizens of America, here is my hand and here is my heart. We will travel to Immanuel's land where sickness, sorrow, pain or death, are feared and felt no more. Then let us come together and strike hands on this union,--and not merely talk about this important union that we have so long wanted and can't do without.

The time will be appointed that we shall have our first meeting. Come on, my friends, from the east and from the west, and from the north and from the south, to the appointed place where union shall fill every breast and be the cry of every heart. There are some of our people that have got so near white that they do not seem to care for their people. Recant this principle, and stamp it under your feet, for there is no good in this order of things. The blood is there and you can't get it away, and you will understand, pure gold is considered better than a mixture, from this draw your ideas, and come along wherever the blood is found and join this united band of colored citizens of America. United we stand, divided we fall. Strife and division have been the downfall of Africa, and it ever has, and ever will be the downfall of any people. Go on in division, and see whether you can ever be exalted as a nation. By this you see the evil that is attached to it. Disunion is the worst thing that ever happened to any nation of people. Look at our present state, and of things in general; for instance, you will look at the churches, if you please; whilst they are in union all things goes well, but as sure as disunion takes place, it seems as if Satan was let loose among the people,--no peace nor satisfaction, and I have thought that the devil was let loose among our people to see them so far from being a united people, not having an eye to that which will make their peace in this world and in the world to come. Come, friends, speak for union one to the other, or

[28]

will you sleep away the time till Jehovah's thunders call you to make peace with all mankind living under heaven, for the day is coming that holiness shall be written on the "bells of the horses,"--"In that day shall there be upon the bells of the horses, HOLINESS UNTO THE LORD." Zechariah xiv. 20. "And they shall teach no more every man his neighbor, and every man his brother, saying, know the Lord: for they shall all know me, from the least of them unto the greatest of them, saith the Lord." Jeremiah xxxi. 34.

Have you any objection to union when you see it has to exist in heaven, when worlds shall exist no more? How long shall it be that this people, who have been great in their time, shall stand so much in their own light? Shall we still endeavor to throw the blame on others, while we will not get right nor do right ourselves? Brethren, we will have to take new steps if we ever expect to please God, for "he that soweth bountifully shall also reap bountifully, and he that soweth sparingly, shall also reap sparingly." Look at the colored citizens of America; I must think that they have sowed more sparingly than any other nation that I can think of at this time, so they are reaping sparingly, just according to the word of God. Look at the nations of the earth, and compare this people with them, and see if they are not sowing sparingly and reaping sparingly. See the houses and farms all in good order. Do they belong to colored citizens? No! and what is the reason that great houses and farms do not belong to some of the colored citizens of America? In the first place, the most of them settle in towns, and there they work every way but the right way. Let us take in consideration some of these ways. In the first place, they let too much of the morning pass away before they get their eyes open. You know that there is no better time to begin a piece of work than in the morning. Well, I have been looking at different towns in America. Who owns all the fine houses? do the colored citizens? No, with few exceptions, you are too idle or too wasteful. With industry, you may have as good a farm as your neighbor's. You may raise as good corn and oats, wheat and barley and rye as any man. The God of heaven sends the rains to water the earth, and my crop is watered with my neighbor. Then, I ask, why are you so far behind? You are to be a nation in time to come, let us be an industrious people.

I recommend the colored citizens of America to turn their attention more to farming than they ever have done. You can have your orchard in a few years, peaches, apples, plums, and all kind of fruit that grows. Not only so, but you can have your cattle,--see the old lady milk the cows in the morning, making ready for breakfast, while the father is looking over the field, and feeding his stock, and the little children as fat as butter. Did you see the large stock of turkies and the large stock of geese? mother raised them all in one year, we shall pluck them and make our beds, and then we shall have feathers to sell that will help father a good deal in his old age. We shall also shear our sheep, and that will be some help. Let us sell some cattle and horses, and buy another farm for James or Nancy, as they are coming up in years and will soon be of age. Take notice, this is all come up from the earth. A good, industrious farmer will soon have all these things and more than I can describe. Then if a farmer's life is so good, it is a wonder that more of those that live in towns do not make their homes in the country. Surely the world is large enough for everybody, and if you cannot get good land at one place you can at another. He that has good land has encouragement. I would not recommend this people to settle on poor ground, like many of the free people in old Virginia and North Carolina, who settled on poor hills that will hardly bring blackberries. There is the state of Illinois; it is a fine country and a free state. And there is the state of Michigan, the finest country likely in America, and many others that I could mention, such as Iowa and Wisconsin. But go and see, and please yourselves, for I am sure that if you are pleased living on land and raising only five or ten bushels of corn to the acre, you would be better pleased by taking your wife and children to a country where you could by the same industry, raise from forty to fifty, or even sixty to eighty bushels of corn to the acre. Then stop dreaming over poor land. Besides all this, farming is the most independent life that a man can live, most especially for the colored citizens of America, who cannot hold any office according to the laws of the different states. But you can hold a farm, more especially if you pay for it, and I am led to believe that it is the greatest office in the United States of America. So I should like to see a number of our people try it and see if it is not a good office. If you are poor, endeavor to earn fifty dollars, and with that fifty dollars you can buy forty acres of land in the new states that I have mentioned.

I have found great fault of our people for the way they put up things about them in building. It seems that if they can just get the cabin to keep the rain out, they don't care how the balance looks. Do have it neat, having a little pride about putting up the cabin, though small. And keep all things nicely that are around, and the blessing of heaven will attend you.

It may be that some of the people may have a desire to know the views that I have concerning this race of people. In the first place, I shall take notice of them in their scattered condition. They are scattered in almost every part of the world--few have houses or lands that are now in the United States and places around; take them in general, they have no home, though born in America. No home! O! is not this race of people to be pitied by all the Christian world? They are in a wandering condition. It puts me in mind of the wandering Israelites, that wandered a lifetime, and had no home. O! where is the heart that cannot not pity this race? Look at the young race, how fast they are rising up; shall they be in the same condition, without homes, wandering about from place to place, learning all kinds of vice? Oh! fathers, has not the God of heaven and earth given you strength and health? Have you not the use of your limbs, the same as other men? Then, I ask, what is the matter that you cannot settle yourselves on farms, buy them, and make homes for your young children that are coming up? I am confident that you can do better than you are doing; some have no home, and yet have been free their lifetime; or it may be, only twenty years, and this day got no home!

How shall this evil be remedied? There is only one cure for it, and that I will mention, hoping the reader will comply with the terms; I am fully convinced, from long experience, of this cure. You tell me that you have been healthy and stout, but you have used all your best days, and have no home; look, and see what is the matter. What is the reason of this sad state of things with this race of people? Some are as hard-working men as ever need be. Can you tell me the reason why you have no home with all your industry? I have looked at the foreigners who have emigrated to this country, looking as though they have not had one dollar in all their lives; and in a few years they have good homes. They seem to be as poor as anybody need to be; some, I see picking up coffee and corn and wheat and all the little sticks of wood that they can find, and carrying them to the place where they live. But stop, in a little time and they have a home; and yet you who were born in America, have no home! Come, friends, it is high time that we should be going to look at these things, and not let every old horse that puts his foot in the path, outrun us. I tell you that there is but one cure for this, and you can be cured if you will comply with instruction. But this disease has been standing a long time, and you know that is the hardest disease to cure. It will take great exertion to break up the disease and cure the patient. He often has this complaint in his feet and in his knees and in his hands, and he can hardly keep his eyes open long enough to tell where his complaint is. No wonder that you are left so far behind; you neither comply, nor tell the complaint; I told you that I felt a little fearful of the old complaints. However, I shall describe one thing, and if that will not do, I do not know what will do. Will you tell me how you feel just at this time, and all your family around you, depending on you to bring something in the house for them? Take notice, you are not getting much by sitting looking into that little fire you have. I have gone all around the complaint, and if you will help me a little, I shall be able to get to the root of this matter; but you must tell me how you felt while I have been going around to get to the matter fully, and make a final cure. I think you can begin to see the complaint, and will

[34]

endeavor to get rid of it as soon as possible; and you can have all things that this earth affords. Rise early, get to business as soon as you can; work late, and be kind and affectionate to your family; do not stand in the streets till it is time for dinner, and then go home and have nothing to eat.

We are lacking on our parts, of the duty that we owe to the Almighty; we can do more than we are doing; for instance, after schooling our children, we can bind them to different trades, so that we may possess among our people all the arts and sciences that man is in possession of. Some of you think you cannot spare your children to go and learn a trade, but you are mistaken; you may have them longer than if they had no trade; for many times your children go to hard servitude on boats or ships, and you never see that son or daughter again. If you had done your duty in giving him a trade, he might set up business in the same city where you live, or travel off to find a better place; and when he has worked long enough to know that it is a better place than where he learned his trade, he goes back and tells them what a fine place he has found, or writes to them to come on where he is. You can either go, or let it alone, but you can see that the child is not exposed to all kinds of danger, as if he had no trade.

Again, it makes better men of them, for boatmen are very apt to be rude. I do not like children to be boatmen; I had rather they should learn every trade under heaven, if some of them have to go on the river or sea to do it. Why should our children stay so far behind others, and you saying you cannot spare them; you are keeping him back; in this way, our nation is kept back. Now let your children learn a trade, or learn to be farmers, and in ten years, you would see a great improvement among this people. Come, friends, let us try it, and then you will see your sons and your daughters come right up from the condition they are in. Let us try it, and never cease till it is accomplished. All heaven is willing for this matter. Who is it that cannot be an honorable man; that is, if he conducts himself in an honorable way? Then seek these things, and they shall come to pass in their season; and if you never seek, you shall never find. Then let every father and every mother and every child seek this principle of honor.

Here we make a severe struggle to bring our race into this honorable society of people; and after we have used all the lawful means that is in our power, then we are to give them up and renounce them, and if he is a thief, let every man, woman and child mark him, and he will not go far, before he is overtaken and put in such close confinement, that he will not disgrace his people. Friends, flesh and blood is nigh, but we must cut ourselves off from everything that is odious in the sight of God and man, in order for this scattered race to redeem themselves from under that heavy frown that looked

[36]

on Africa, when she transgressed against God, and fell from the state she was then in. And great was the fall! yes, so great that man can feel it to this day; and them that look upon her condition, mourn her sad condition. We sprang from that nation, and shall we still disobey, and never come from that fallen state? Brethren, let us come together and search out the cursed thing that keeps us so far back in this world.

Let us try ourselves by the standard of truth, and still call on the God of heaven and earth to help us in our sad condition. O, that a strong union may exist in every breast, in order that we may have this union complete, as God requires it to be.

We call on the people in the name of our God, to give themselves to fasting and prayer on Easter Monday; let it be a solemn day that we set apart from all other days, all through our lives, and then as long as time shall be, or till the sun shall be blown out, to rise no more. Then our day of fasting and prayer comes to an end, and we will be gathered home; they that have done good, to the resurrection of life; and they that have done evil, to the resurrection of damnation; all will be brought forth, then, in their own order. Let this day of fasting and prayer be remembered by all on earth, and nations unborn may rise up and hold this day that is set apart by their fathers in 1847.

[37]

The day chosen is Easter Monday, in the year 1847; that all churches, of every name and every order under heaven, are called upon to give that day to the Lord our God, in fasting and prayer, for the union of this people that they shall no longer live at a distance from their God, and from each other. O, that every soul that has set his foot on God Almighty's footstool, may claim that day to be a day of days to his soul! Saint and sinner are called upon this day, so long as the Lord your God gives you breath to breathe, and the time rolls around, and you find yourself in existence. Who knows, what God may do for you, when millions are engaged the same day and time, calling on God for a union. He may unite your soul to Christ by a living faith. Do not neglect it--now is your time--God says, try me and prove me, and see if I do not pour you out such a blessing, that there shall not be room enough to receive it. Brethren, prayer and fasting have removed mountains. When we look at God, we must look at him just as he is, a God of all power and all goodness, love and mercy; and this is all for man. If they will ask for it they shall have it, and more, in this life, and in the world to come, life everlasting; then let us believe in him and ask for the things we need.

When Mordecai perceived all that was done, he rent his clothes, and put on sackcloth with ashes, and went into the midst of the city, and cried with a loud and a bitter cry, for he knew that they were in a dreadful condition, from the decree that had gone out from the king, that every Jew should be destroyed. This went through all the provinces whosesoever the king had command. Surely, this rested heavy on the minds of the Jews--they proclaimed a day of fasting and prayer. It seems that every Jew was in the same condition that lived in the king's provinces. Well, they cried with Mordecai, and united their cries to the Lord, the God of heaven and earth; and this cry came to the queen, and she was a Jewess; and when Mordecai brought it to her understanding, that though she was Queen Esther, she was a Jewess, and had to die with her people, then she increased the fasting and praying threefold; for she and her maidens fasted and prayed three days and three nights. Although it was death to enter the king's inner court, yet she arose and said, if I perish, I perish; and she dressed herself in royal apparel, and went into the inner court, and the king held out the sceptre to her. Thus was she made instrumental in the hands of God, of turning the king's fury, and granting liberty to the Jews. O, can we not trust God for all things, and go to work like men that belong to the Lord Our God? You see this great deliverance that the Lord our God hath wrought for the Jews. He is no respecter of persons, of those that put their trust in him. Let us take God at his word; watch and pray, that ye enter not into temptation. You will recollect that Jonah was not delivered from the whale's belly, until he had prayed and entered into covenant with

God, and agreed to do that thing which the Lord had commanded him to do; then the God of the sea and land commanded the fish to take him to shore. It seems that there must be an unwillingness in man, to do what God intends he shall do; and if he still hardens his heart, he has great reason to fear the judgments of the Almighty; and it seems to me, that the judgments of God are upon this nation, and it becomes us to begin to ask of God what he will have us to do. Let all ask, and not only ask, but let us mend our ways while we are asking of our heavenly Father. I find, while Jonah prayed, his heart became more humble; he says he was in pain. When God Almighty threatened Nineveh with an overthrow for their transgressions, did they stand idle after they got the word from the man of God? No! but they come down immediately, even in dust and ashes before God; fasted, prayed, and God's wrath was appeased. Ask, and it shall be given.

The day that was set that we should hold apart unto the Lord, is come; it has found me on God Almighty's footstool, with the breath of life in me. Shall I be one that shall, in the hand of God, be a helper to consecrate this day to the Lord our God, by giving myself to the Lord in fasting and prayer, with all this great body of people that shall this day unite their cries around the throne of God, our Saviour, praying that the God of heaven and earth may grant us united prayerful hearts, all the days of our lives. O that my heart and soul may be warm with this united prayer, that never was called on before, particularly for this people, in their situation. O Lord, help us now to call on thee, our God, to assist each one upon thy footstool, on land or on rivers, on the ocean or wherever the day may find them; may they not be of a stubborn heart on that day, and cause God Almighty's anger to wax hot against them, because they have no desire to forsake their idols, and call on the name of the Lord our God.

One day, when Cornelius fasted and prayed, God heard and answered, and said he was "no respecter of persons, but in every nation, he that feareth him and worketh righteousness, is accepted with him." Acts x. 34. Fasting and prayer is a righteous act before God.

What shall a man give in exchange for his soul? The soul of man, according to the word of God, is always sensible of what state it is in, whether in hell or heaven, or on earth. Had I a million of worlds, would I not give them all to know, in my last hours in this world, that I had made my peace with my creator, God? Time is leaving you; consider, you have only one life and one soul, and you may throw it into hell or heaven by your conduct in this life. The soul is sensible after death. "Turn ye unto me, saith the Lord of hosts, and I will turn to you." The Lord calls man to turn his course, and he will meet him by turning to him.

Malachi, chap. x. 2, says, "If ye will not hear and if ye will not lay it to heart to give glory unto my name, saith the Lord of hosts, I will even send a curse upon you, and will curse your blessings; yea, I have cursed them already, because ye do not lay it to heart." O, will this people stand idle, without thought? shall they let time move them into eternity, to face the very God that made them, and bade them call, and they have refused the call? Look what you are doing by refusing the call of God Almighty; you are sealing your own damnation, and making sure your own destruction. Do you say, I have no time to repent? I tell you, before God and all the angels that surround the throne, you may be in hell before to-morrow morning! Then be sure that you do not neglect your soul till it is too late. One generation is passing away, and another is rising up; at last, all will pass away at one time. Now, among the eight hundred millions that inhabit this globe, thirty and three years, or thereabouts takes them into eternity, and others rise up and take their place, and in the same time this generation passes away to their long home. I want you to understand that it takes about the time mentioned, for one generation to pass away. If a generation passes away in thirty-three years, how many generations must have passed already into another world!

And these unnumbered millions, at the sound of the trump of God, have to come to the judgment seat of Christ, and every one to answer for the deeds done in the body, good or bad. O, heaven enable us to have good deeds, that we may answer with joy and not with grief. Millions of those born again, will see their father's face, in that blessed world of rest that is prepared for them. O come, and let us try this new birth that Christ taught to Nicodemus; "you must be born again, or you cannot see the kingdom of God." O come, and let us seal our everlasting peace by obeying the voice of God, whilst we have ears to hear, or a heart to understand! O praise the Lord for his goodness, that he ever stooped so low as to give his only begotten Son to make atonement for us, that whosoever believed in him, though he was dead, he should be made alive! Every sinner has a dead soul in him, and that dead soul must be made alive, or burn in hell to all eternity. Attend to it! Death will soon move that dead soul to its place. Death has to kill the body, that the soul may no longer have a hiding place in this house of clay. Death has shattered the soul's cabin, in which the soul dwelleth, and it is compelled to leave. It is naked because it hath not sought any covering of the Maker of heaven and earth. For this reason it is a naked and dead soul, out of its shelter. Death came across its cabin, and tore it down; and the soul cannot build it again, for death did not come till he got permission from his master; he generally fights the body, and he gets it worried down lower and

[43]

lower, until the soul must leave, because of death. Where must it go? It is naked! it is not covered with the righteousness of Christ! Then, according to the Book of God, it must be exposed to every evil spirit, and be seized by them, and brought down to that world of woe and misery, where the fallen angels are confined in chains of darkness, until the Day of the Judgment of the great God Almighty! Then they will hear their final doom.

O, do not let the judgment find the soul unprepared! Feet, where are you carrying the soul to? are you not walking in forbidden paths? Death may be in some of these paths. Hands, how often have you warred against the soul, doing the very thing that God hath forbidden? Mouth, have you not helped to damn the soul, by cursing and swearing and lying? All these things lead down to the pit of damnation. Eyes, what are you about, that you cannot watch for the soul, and not suffer these feet and hands and mouth to do so much mischief to the soul? because, if you do not watch these many members, they will damn the soul to all eternity. It seems that the tongue is an unruly member; James says, "it cannot be tamed; it is unruly, and full of deadly poison; set on fire of hell." Cannot the eye watch the other members, and keep them from damning the soul, by running headlong into forbidden paths? I condemn all the members, eye, hand and foot; they are all agreed together, to go on and war against the soul. Then the mind must be

[44]

changed. God keep thy tongue from evil, and thy lips from speaking guile.

It is out of the abundance of the heart that the mouth speaketh, and with the heart men believe unto righteousness, and with the mouth confession is made unto salvation. These things do not war against the soul; you have fruit unto holiness, and the end is everlasting life. How much better, then, it is to endeavor to save the soul! Let the same mind be in you that was in Christ Jesus, and endeavor to be led by the Spirit of Christ; for if any man have not the Spirit of Christ he is none of his. The Holy Spirit does a great deal; he frees the soul, calms the burning flames and brings the dead soul to life. He provides a heavenly garment, so that when death comes, it may kill the body, but it cannot kill the soul, because of the blood of Christ. So much, then, for having the mind of Christ. Let all seek to have the mind changed, that we may be led by the Spirit of Christ. In order to be led by the Spirit of Christ, we must be born again; born of that spirit that can lead us from earth to that blessed world of rest, that remains for the people of God.

Come, friends, don't read, and do no more. You must make the inquiry, how stands the case between God Almighty and your soul; and endeavor to receive the Spirit of Christ, that you may be a lively stone in the building, meet for the master's use, cleansed by his blood! A lively stone in the

[45]

building? We must live godly and soberly in Christ Jesus the Lord, which is your salvation.

Now, I leave this part in your minds, till I look over the world of mankind, and see how many there are that will take heed to their way, and come up unitedly to serve the Lord with one accord, and be the people God wants them to be. For he says, "Ethiopia shall soon stretch out her hands unto God." Look, now, and see if you are making any exertion in this matter. God has said it, and you must do it, and do it unitedly; for he judges Israel, and kill them that would not obey. O, Ethiopia, have you obeyed the voice of God Almighty, that spoke by the voice of thunder, to the Israelites on the Mount Sinai? They saw the cloud, and heard the thunder so loud, that they feared to stand near, but told Moses to go and speak to God; and all that God told him they should do, did they do it? No, but still rebelled against the man of God, and refused to take the counsel that God gave to Moses for them. For this, the Lord's anger was kindled against Israel, and he made them wander in the wilderness forty years, until the generation that had done evil in the sight of the Lord was consumed. Then be not an evil doer, lest thou share the same fate. Many things that we do can be let alone; do you believe it? then let alone evil practices; the mind must be changed before you can be saved. "The Spirit and the bride say, Come. And let him that heareth say, Come. And let him that is athirst come. And whosoever will, let him take of the water of life freely."--Rev. xxii. 17.

I have heard some people say that at God's own appointed time he would bring all these things to pass that we have been speaking about. Friends, let me tell you the truth, and you believe it, God's time is when you get right and do right. God ever has worked in this way with the nations of the earth, so you need not to think of living in your laziness, never asking God to help and bless you and your family, but still say that God will do all at his appointed time. That appointed time is now, this day. God told Noah to build the ark, and he went to work and built it. The same God has told you to repent of your sins. Have you done so? The same God told Israel what they had to do before they left Egypt. Were they obedient to God's word or not? God does not bless men in disobedience. In order that we may receive strength from the Lord our God, we must be obedient to him as the Governor of the universe. Whatever he bids us do hasten so to do, as obedient children, and not set on the stool of do nothing saying, that God in his own appointed time will bring all things to pass as though he did not require any thing of you at all. My friend, if you look at it just as it is, God has laid the foundation and you are the builders. Now tell me what are you waiting for? God has done his work in laying the foundation and tells you to build on the foundation: "for other foundation can no man lay than that is laid, which is Jesus Christ." 1 Cor. iii. 11. God requires to use all the means in our power to bring peace and union, that God's name may be glorified here on the earth. How are men to build on the foundation that God has laid? They should "seek, first the kingdom of God, and his righteousness; and all these things shall be added unto you." Matthew vi. 33. Then God looks for your work. You are not your own, you are bought with a price, and of course have to work for him that bought you with his own precious blood. He redeemed us for himself. Then let us begin a heavenly work, having an eye particularly on this young race, and give them to the Lord our God, in prayer, even as Hannah gave Samuel to the Lord. She said, "I have lent him to the Lord; as long as he liveth he shall be lent to the Lord." 1 Samuel i. 28. O then, if we have that desire to see a generation rising from the dust, clothed with the righteousness of the Lord our God, let us do as Hannah did, give them to God Almighty. Pray for them, and pray with them; send them to Sunday school, and train them up to God in their young days. Then all will unite in the same thing, and then you will see the nation that God Almighty will delight to own and bless.

Many of the colored people are free, and have neither master nor owner. Then surely you can train up your children in the way they should go, and when they grow old they will not depart from it. If you fail to do what is in your power to do with these children how can you look for a blessing. In time past, your fathers were deprived of this blessing, and of course they could not be charged with not raising their children in the right manner; that is, if they did all they could according to their situation. But as you are free, (thanks be to God for it,) the guilt comes on your own head. Industry and education should be your concern about this young race. Look over the whole world, and see the nations all endeavoring to advance to a higher state of life. Industry and good education is the principal way of advancing in life. Look at the Friends or Quakers. They go on with steady habits. All things are clean and nice around them. They raise their children to be industrious and give them a good education. Can we not take pattern by them? Move on in the circle of life patiently, making but little noise. Always keep at work but never seem to be in a hurry. Don't work a great deal one or two days and then loiter three or four days. My friend, you must have another spirit in you, or the little spirit that is in you must be kindled up. You have lived here long enough to have had a good house and home, then had buildings to rent out. Instead of that, you are getting old, and have not a house to put your head in. I think if you would live a little more plain and save some of your money, you might in time be able to buy yourself a good farm. There are very few of our people that have their own house to live in. They generally live in rented houses or on rented farms. Is there no help for this? I should work night and day, and never stop till I got a piece of land to build a house on. Industry and care will do it. Don't get out of heart, and go and get drunk before you buy your land. I hope that you will consider that just as long as you are living in rented houses you are making yourself a slave for somebody else, and you say you do not like slavery. You say that you are free and have been so for many years, and have paid money enough to have bought a good house and lot. Friends, these things ought not so to be. They can be altered. I tell you perseverance will alter them. Try it, and I do not think you will ever regret it. Then why set ye here and look at one another? Why not get enough to last as long as you and all your family live. Don't sit there any longer. Rise and go to work like men, and buy property and live like men and women in this world. If you have not got religion, God sends rain on the just and the unjust. But while you are receiving all these good things, remember, O man, that thou hast an immortal soul that has to be saved or lost to all eternity. Then let us wake up, not only in regard to earthly concerns, but also in regard to eternity, which is just before us. While we are gathering earthly things take notice that there are heavenly things that can be gathered that will last in that blessed world where God has a house not made with hands, eternal in the heavens. Come, come, you that read this little book,--think, that your eyes look upon it now, but in a little time the eyes that see it will be closed in death, and where will the soul be? We have taught you the way of life in this little book, and if you take the word of life your soul will be forever blessed of the Lord our God. We have taught you the word that was good for soul and body, and after all, if you refuse it, O let me tell you, you refuse the salvation of your own soul. I have laid before you many temporal enjoyments that are calculated to make a man see many good days in this world, but to prepare for death is better than all things besides, because this life is not long, but the life to come has no end. Come then and learn to fear the Lord, that your days may be long. But spend your time in laboring and attend to your own business and be saving of all that the Lord enables you to get. Use much industry, and you will see in a little time if you will not have as good a home as any man.

I call industry, King Cure-all, and I call idleness, Mr. Pull-down-all. Notice, every industrious man must be happy, if he have a good industrious, saving wife; that man surely will have him a home; then he will have no need of working for everybody but himself. In a few years, with care, he will have a farm or a ship or a boat; but the farm before all. A good industrious farmer, surely has the greatest enjoyment of any situation in life. It is a desirable situation for any good man. A bad man does not care for the things that will make him happy, and all around him. A good industrious man will be respected by all that know him; he has no

[51]

stingy principle, but always ready to bear a hand to any good thing; nice in his family, nice in dealing and in all his deportment.

I will give you a description of King Cure-all and Mr. Pull-down-all. King Cure-all is much of a gentleman; his word is good for all that he tells you; you need not fear him, for I have known him for about fifty years, and I never knew him to fail in anything. He is a great man. You can try him; he will soon give you land, or a good home. He is very rich, and never fails to give to everyone that goes to him; he will not only give you land, but he will also give you horses and cattle, and sheep and hogs, and geese and turkeys, and more than I can mention at this time; he has plenty for every one that goes to him; he keeps all things nice around him; you can go into his house any day, and you will see all the things setting in their right places. Go into his field, you will see his nice farm and good fences, and good barn, for that is half the battle with King Cure-all. This barn enables him to keep the things that he raises on his farm, and to pick up the crumbs, that nothing be lost. King Cure-all is a mighty man; he has plenty of money to give to everyone that comes; he has a good many friends, and they are generally wealthy-Sir, if you do not belong to that class, and have not been to see the gentleman, I would recommend you to come immediately. His acquaintance is large; his friends sometimes have to share the fate of all the earth, by that monster called

[52]

death, which takes both young and old. They generally make a will, and will the fine things received from King Cure-all, to his friends; and it may be, if you go and get well acquainted with him, some of his friends may will you a large amount some of these days. So; I should sweep my house right clean, set down and talk with my wife and children about the matter, and make the agreement to take wife and children along, to see King Cure-all. Friend, you have now started with your whole family, to see the gentleman; I hope that you will excuse me, if I give you a little advice, while you and your family are on the way. You have made a lively start--you have swept your house clean and nice--you are on the way; go on, and take care that you do not get drunk before you get to your journey's end. If you follow that practice, you can never see King Cure-all; a drunken man does not get much of his fortune. If he should happen to get hold of some, he generally takes it away again. Only think, how awful it looks, to see a man start to see a gentleman, from whom he expects to receive support for all his family, and just before he arrives in sight of King Cure-all, he gets drunk and turns back! O, how awful is drunkenness! It has made many lose their health and all their property. No man need ever expect to arrive at any honorable station in life, that uses any intoxicating drink. His children's bread is gone!--he has left his wife to mourn!--his strength decays!--O, how dreadful it appears! Mothers, don't you feel the sting of this

[53]

one thing? Is there no way that these things may be moved from the nation. May God help each man and woman and child to decide this matter this day, that they will be no longer one of the subjects of Alcohol.

Now, I will give you a description of Mr. Pull-down-all, with his laziness. I called him a gentleman; I hope that you will excuse me, for I perceive that I called him altogether out of his name, for he seems always to be shuffling about in the way. I cannot tell anything good about him, for he runs about from house to house; he has nothing, and gets nothing, unless he steals it; for his laziness pesters him so, that he can hardly live; and I am surprised that he has existed so long. King Cure-all's friends have given him a large amount, but he soon wastes all; there is neither care nor decency in him; it is a wonder that dirt has not killed him long ago. Did you ever go into his house? If you have not, I have, and I never saw anything clean about his house. Well, I think laziness is the worst thing in the world, and Mr. Pull-down-all has plenty of that. His looks show it; look how dirty and ragged he keeps himself and family. Do you not think, if he was a working man, that he could keep himself and family a little nicer? The wife, I think, might keep herself a little better; I think, likely, laziness has got hold of her also. No wonder, then, that the house is dirty, and the children are ragged. I can't tell any more about Mr. Pull-down-all, but do keep out of his company, or else he will pull you down. Come, friends, we must wake up, for it is high time that the things which have so long kept us back, should be thrown aside, and we go on for better things.

"Better things!" says Mr. Pull-down. I thought that I would not have anything more to say about Mr. Pull-down, but seeing you have asked the question, and seem as if you were surprised that we have a desire to go on for better things, I shall give a little further detail of your character. It seems to me, that you are perfectly satisfied in the situation that you have kept your family in all the days of your life, and you are not willing to make any improvement. You have been so long a pulling down, that you think that is the best way for you. Do you see what a bad character you have? Besides, this does not stop with you; for here are the children, whose characters you are pulling down by your conduct; you will not work yourself, nor teach your children to work, and use all industry, that they might be a blessing to their people. All that you care for in this life, is to live from hand to mouth, and learning your children the same way. I have been looking at this state of things many years, and have thought, if you would only let the bottle go, and take that money that has kept you and all your family back, that it would be a great gain to you and all around you. If you will live in your dirt and laziness, all that we can do, is to make the division that was spoken of before in this little book. How

[55]

are we ever to raise up an honorable set of colored citizens in America, if we do not take our children in hand, and show them the way.

We are desirous to have all the children in school, but you say, No. If we cannot carry the whole race along, we will carry just as many as we can get to join the army of King Cure-all. He has been already described.

In thinking what is best for this people, I have been thinking that it would be best to obey the word of God. God has taken great pains to show man his will, concerning one day of the seven, called the Sabbath, or the Lord's day. This is the day that God has blessed, and taken to himself, and told us to keep it holy. You will have to answer at the bar of God, how you have spent your Sabbaths. God has commanded you to keep them holy. Have you done so? In Genesis, second chapter and third verse, we read, "And God blessed the seventh day, and sanctified it, because that in it he had rested from all his works which God created and made." You see, that the day is blessed by the God that made it. Again, in Exodus, twentieth chapter and ninth verse, see how careful the Lord is, in telling you what time is allowed to man, for his earthly concerns; "Six days shalt thou labor and do all thy work." I ask the reader, is thy labor done in six days? Hark, the voice of God is, Exodus XX. 10, "The seventh day is the Sabbath of the Lord thy God: In it thou shalt not do any work, thou, nor thy son, nor thy daughter, thy man-servant, nor thy maid-servant, nor thy cattle, nor thy stranger that is within thy gates." This is the word of God. See how strict he is, in giving you directions how you should conduct yourself. Will you still go on, abusing that holy day, till the God of heaven calls you to the judgment-seat of Christ? How long will you disobey the voice of God, and still look for his blessings to raise you from your state of degradation? He must see a disposition in you to do his will, and then you may look for the blessing of the Great Head of the Church upon you, in copious showers.

In my travels, I saw a colored man, that stated to me, that he had not had one meal's victuals cooked in his house for twenty-five years, on the Sabbath day. I stayed in his house one week. He is, at this time, worth about fifteen thousand dollars; he has been baptized, and seems to be very pious. You had just as well cook your victuals on Saturday, for Sunday, as to break the Lord's day cooking, and giving great dinners to your friends. Let us be more strict about these things.

Look how many Sunday schools there are in America. Our white friends have established many Sunday schools for colored children, but some fathers and mothers are so little concerned for the welfare of their children, that they do not send them. If God has given our white friends grace to

[57]

establish Sunday schools for your children, I should think that you ought to have grace enough to send them. May God Almighty bless them abundantly for their good work. Come, then, old and young, and let us attend the Sunday school.

So, my friends, we will go on to do our duty as far as we can to the whole race of mankind. We have agreed to unite, one with another, to endeavor to raise up this young generation; to take our place in love and union among them in this world. We think that the Lord hath commanded, and he will bring to pass.

This united band of brethren can and must make some regulation for raising the little ones that are under our protection. I talked about a division, but if we can get laziness out of the way, there need be no division; for we are determined, henceforth, to lead an honorable life. We have, already, as honorable men as the world affords, in their station; but this united band of brethren has a heart, feeling desire to see the whole race of free people united in one band, that they may instruct their children, and receive instruction one from another. O, then, this union; let it come, and fill the whole earth! How good and how pleasant it is, when brethren all agree! Come along, my dear friend, we have no desire to leave one behind. But, sir, if you will not come and join this honorable society, and endeavor to live an honorable life, we must leave you; for this united band do not intend to hold a dishonorable person in their society; for I want you to know, that at this time, we, as free people, have the raising of our own children, and we are called to our duty.

Brethren and friends that are now in America, on land or seas, on rivers or lakes, or all below the sun, your warmest attention is called to awake up to this laudable work. Oh, will you come and help us in this great work? Lay hand and heart to work, and may God roll on a full union among this people, when they shall all seek the same thing, and be willing to join together, and be a heart-feeling people, joined in one solid band of union, never to be broken, till the sun shall rise and set no more. O, that God would write every name in heaven that joins this United Band of Colored Citizens of America; for our hearts are engaged before God, to give our children to the Lord our God, that we may raise an honorable nation. This old people must be engaged night and day, for we have lost too much time. We might have had this good work going on long ago, had we had moral courage enough to take this in hand. And, as we are determined to look more diligently into this, amongst a multitude of counselors there is safety; and we shall be safe, if we do what God Almighty has told us to do; namely, train up the child for God Almighty's own use; he will make the man of him. We feel for this great mass of young people, growing up without homes; and we think, and are sure, that by taking

[59]

them in hand, giving them a good education, and learning them habits of industry in a manual labor school, that thousands of them may be put in the way to have good homes. I shall leave this subject with you, feeling that you like to have smart children, that can attend to business.

I think, of all people under heaven, this people has the greatest right to endeavor to improve their minds and themselves in general, for the great work of God Almighty; and how can this general improvement take place, except we become united, and then form such regulations that actually will be a benefit to the whole nation.

Then let every state and county, and town and village, wherever the colored man is, below the sun, and he is free, I say again and again, let them choose them a man or men, and send on to the great NATIONAL CONVENTION that shall be held in the year of our Lord, 1847, time and place mentioned after this; for there must be a general meeting of this people, before we can accomplish this union that has to be accomplished, before we need to open our mouths about elevation or honor, or the general education of the youth.

Then, let each state or county, or city or village, or town or any place below the sun, send a man or men to represent them to the convention. I say again, that they should hold meetings with each other, in the different places mentioned, and see if this union could not be accomplished, in order to let the convention know that this union can be accomplished.

I say again, that all those different societies, and every name and order, without respect of persons, may send from their different stations, a letter to the convention, and that letter shall certify that they certainly do see and feel the need of this union, and to let the convention know, that your hearts and souls feel, to be united to the great United Band of Colored Citizens of America. Then send your letters, with the pledge. All those letters should be kept in good order by the convention, and ordered to be bound in a book, that the rising generation may hear about the great meeting of their aged fathers. They will hear how their fathers came together on that day, and presented their names and pledges, to be united to the great body of colored citizens, that are now free. Colored men of America, wherever you are scattered in different directions upon American soil, prepare for this great meeting. Oh, that God would enable all free people to send their man or men, to the National Convention! Send your name, and place of residence, with your desire and pledge, that the same may be recorded in the great Ledger that shall be handed down from generation to generation. Then shall they remember that this nation has made agreement before God and angels, that this union shall exist till the sun shall rise and set no more forever. Amen! Even so! Come, Lord Jesus, and help this people to stretch out their hands unto God.

Again, by your sending a letter we shall know that a union is already formed as to your part. The record shall be made according to your desire. So send the desire of your soul. May the God of heaven and earth enable you all to live in peace and union from this time until the tongue is still in death.

Particular pains should be taken how you speak to each other, and to everybody, for if we are going to make an improvement, we should improve the whole man. So I am for making an improvement in our words. Let even the thought of this union, never to be broken, cause wrath to cease, and bitter words to be thrown away like the chaff of the summer threshing floor.

Dear friends, this little book is now coming to a close. I pray that God may open the hearts of all who read this little book for the reception of the things written in it.

But before I close these remarks, I shall call on all the females that live this side of the haven of eternal rest. You expect to rest your soul in glory in a coming day; do you not wish to meet your children there? I call on you to let the God of heaven rule your judgment in this great work, for I do assure you that it is your children that the God of heaven hath put it in our hearts to endeavor to unite in one band of union, in order that we may give a general education to this young race, without respect of persons, so we call on you to assist us by lending your aid in this matter. Much may be done by you in carrying on this great work. O then, let young and old say, seeing that God hath spared my life to see these days come, I will and this union band. Then, sisters, form yourselves in bands. Call them union bands, and meet once a month and bring something with you, and all put your mites together for a school fund. Then the convention will not have to wait till one year before they can begin their operations, but they can say in the convention where they will establish the first school, appoint men to attend the work, and go right on and raise schools. You can then send your children to a school of your own, and have them well taken care of. It makes no matter where they come from, all will be treated alike, all sleep alike, all eat alike. I have the opinion that it would be better for children to move them to different schools, so soon as we could get them in order to receive children; my opinion is, that pious teachers would be the best for these schools.

I cannot close before I give a general call to the colored citizens of America to attend the NATIONAL CONVENTION IN PITTSBURGH, on the first Monday in September, 1847.

[63]

A resolution was passed at the convention of colored ministers, held in Philadelphia, in July, 1846, appointing a committee to call a National Convention to take into consideration the general education of our youth, and also the general union of those free people of color that are now scattered in different directions in the United States of America. The names of the committee calling the Convention are the following:--

- JOHN B. MEACHUM, St. Louis, Mo.
- WILLIAM WILLIAMS, Washington, D. C.
- JEREMIAH ASHER, Providence, R. I.
- JAMES Mc C. CRUMMILL, Philadelphia, Pa.

The committee calls upon all the free colored citizens of the United States. It is an especial call for the union of this great body of people. Do not fail to come, all of every name and order, far and wide. Send your man or men, to show that your heart hath joined that body of colored citizens. Our souls shall cry for union from one end of the globe to the other as far as an Ethiopian's foot has trod the soil, and the news reaches the ear.

We are going to come together in the year of our Lord 1847, on the first Monday in September. We shall endeavor to form plans, and establish manual labor schools in different directions, wherever the convention thinks most expedient. Let

[64]

this union be formed and the representatives strike hands and hearts together. Let us form a union that never shall be dissolved so long as the sun and moon and stars shall move on; when all these give up their courses and fall from their places then our union will cease in this world, but then we shall go to join that great company that is spoken of in Revelation.

In order that we should not wait a year before we begin operations, let us be active about this matter. It is surely worth your notice. Begin now to hold your meetings and put all your pennies together, and send them by the man that you send to the Convention. If all will do this, when the Convention breaks up, then those who may be appointed by the Convention to attend to this business, can begin immediately. Do not fail to send your mites, for we have lost too much time already. Friends, work a little harder.

Certainly, the MOTHERS of the children will wake up on this matter. The ladies can do a great deal if they form themselves into circles, and pay in school funds. And the YOUNG MEN should form themselves into companies called the United Band, and raising this school fund, and in a little time, the school will start, and then you can have the privilege of going to this school. And in a little time, we will have some kinds of trades going on there, and you can have the privilege of learning a

[65]

good trade, and getting a good education at the same time.

Do not fail to pray that God would bless the deliberations of the Convention, so that the temporal and spiritual welfare of our race may be secured, and the glory of God promoted.

NATIONAL CONVENTION.

The National Convention of the Colored citizens of America, will be held in PITTSBURG, on the first Monday in September, 1847.

www.ingramcontent.com/pod-product-compliance
Lightning Source LLC
La Vergne TN
LVHW052038080426
835513LV00018B/2381